W9-AAZ-104

Mapping the Continents

Mapping Africa

Paul Rockett

✦

with artwork by Mark Ruffle

Crabtree Publishing Company

www.crabtreebooks.com

Crabtree Publishing Company
www.crabtreebooks.com
1-800-387-7650

Published in Canada
616 Welland Ave.
St. Catharines, ON
L2M 5V6

Published in the United States
PMB 59051, 350 Fifth Ave.
59th Floor,
New York, NY

Published in 2017 by CRABTREE PUBLISHING COMPANY.

All rights reserved. No part of this publication may be reproduced, stored in a retrieval system or be transmitted in any form or by any means, electronic, mechanical, photocopying, recording, or otherwise, without the prior written permission of the copyright owner.

First published in 2015 by The Watts Publishing Group (An imprint of Hachette Children's Group)
Copyright © The Watts Publishing Group 2015

Author: Paul Rockett

Editorial director: Kathy Middleton

Editors: Adrian Cole, and Ellen Rodger

Proofreader: Wendy Scavuzzo

Series design and illustration:
Mark Ruffle, www.rufflebrothers.com

Prepress technician: Katherine Berti

Print and production coordinator: Katherine Berti

Printed in Canada/072016/PB20160525

Picture credits:
Catalan Atlas 1375, detail: 9tr; Ulrich Doering/Alamy: 16t; Great Stock PL/Alamy: 22b; Justin Hall, Culver City/Wikimedia Commons: 14bl; Bruno de Hogues/Gettyimages: 27c; l'Illustration/ Wikimedia Commons: 10cr; imageBroker/Alamy: 13br; Anton Ivanov/Shutterstock: 19t; jelldragon/Alamy: 13cr; Eric Laffourgue/ Alamy: 24t; Marka/Alamy: 18b; Wayne Parsons/Getty Images: 20b; Photosky/Dreamstime: 17b; Photogenes: 27t; Patrick Poendi/ Dreamstime: 12tr; Princeton University: 4b; Temps/Shutterstock: 17t; Tommy Trenchard/Alamy: 22c; Watchtheworld/Shutterstock: 18t; Wikimedia Commons: flags; Worldshots/Dreamstime: 23b.

Every attempt has been made to clear copyright. Should there by any inadvertent omission please apply to the publisher for rectification.

Library and Archives Canada Cataloguing in Publication

Rockett, Paul, author
    Mapping Africa / Paul Rockett.

(Mapping the continents)
Includes index.
Issued in print and electronic formats.
ISBN 978-0-7787-2612-8 (hardback).--
ISBN 978-0-7787-2618-0 (paperback).--
ISBN 978-1-4271-1779-3 (html)

    1. Africa--Juvenile literature. 2. Cartography--Africa--Juvenile literature. 3. Africa--Geography--Juvenile literature. 4. Africa-- Description and travel--Juvenile literature. 5. Africa--Maps--Juvenile literature. I. Title.

DT3.R64 2016   j916   C2016-902650-7
                                            C2016-902651-5

Library of Congress Cataloging-in-Publication Data

Names: Rockett, Paul, author.
Title: Mapping Africa / Paul Rockett.
Description: New York : Crabtree Publishing Company, 2016. | Series: Mapping the continents | Includes index.
Identifiers: LCCN 2016016672 (print) | LCCN 2016020770 (ebook) | ISBN 9780778726128 (reinforced library binding) | ISBN 9780778726180 (pbk.) | ISBN 9781427117793 (electronic HTML)
Subjects: LCSH: Africa--Juvenile literature. | Cartography--Africa--Juvenile literature. | Africa--Geography--Juvenile literature. | Africa--Description and travel--Juvenile literature.
Classification: LCC DT3 .R64 2016 (print) | LCC DT3 (ebook) | DDC 916--dc23
LC record available at https://lccn.loc.gov/2016016672

Contents

Where is Africa?

Africa is the second-largest continent in the world. Its landmass covers more than one fifth of Earth's surface. Its mainland is connected to Asia by a narrow stretch of land, while large oceans and sea surround the rest of the continent.

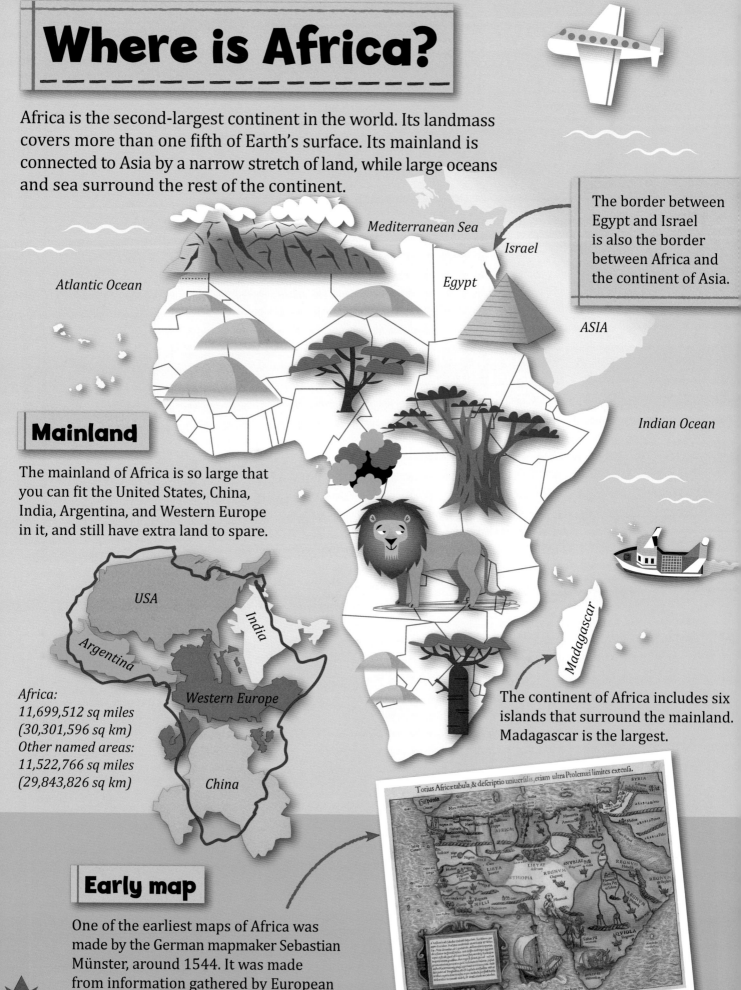

Mediterranean Sea

Israel

Atlantic Ocean

Egypt

The border between Egypt and Israel is also the border between Africa and the continent of Asia.

ASIA

Indian Ocean

Mainland

The mainland of Africa is so large that you can fit the United States, China, India, Argentina, and Western Europe in it, and still have extra land to spare.

USA

India

Argentina

Western Europe

China

Africa:
11,699,512 sq miles
(30,301,596 sq km)
Other named areas:
11,522,766 sq miles
(29,843,826 sq km)

Madagascar

The continent of Africa includes six islands that surround the mainland. Madagascar is the largest.

Early map

One of the earliest maps of Africa was made by the German mapmaker Sebastian Münster, around 1544. It was made from information gathered by European explorers, and much of it was incorrect.

The equator

The **equator** is an imaginary line running around the middle of Earth, halfway between the North Pole and the South Pole. It divides Earth into the Northern **Hemisphere** and the Southern Hemisphere.

The equator runs through the African countries of Gabon, Republic of the Congo, Democratic Republic of the Congo, Uganda, Kenya, and Somalia.

The tropics

The **tropics** are imaginary lines that run around Earth where temperatures are high all year round.

The Tropic of Cancer runs around Earth about 23.5 degrees north of the equator, and goes through the African countries of Morocco, the **member state** of Western Sahara, Mauritania, Mali, Algeria, Niger, Libya, Chad, and Egypt.

The Tropic of Capricorn runs about 23.5 degrees south of the equator, and goes through the African countries of Namibia, Botswana, South Africa, Mozambique, and Madagascar.

Tropic of Cancer

Equator

Tropic of Capricorn

Locating Africa

We can describe the location of Africa in relation to the areas of land and water that surround it, and using the points on a compass.

N

W   E

S

Europe   Asia

Atlantic
Ocean

Africa

Indian
Ocean

- Africa is west of Asia

- Africa is south of Europe

- Africa is between the Atlantic Ocean and the Indian Ocean

5

Countries

Africa is made up of 54 countries and one member state—more countries than any other continent. It has the second-largest population of all the continents after Asia, and it is home to more than 1 billion people.

Regions

When people talk about places in Africa, they often refer to them by geographical region. These regions are North Africa, West Africa, Central Africa, East Africa, and Southern Africa. Southern Africa refers to the southern part of the continent, and should not be confused with the country South Africa.

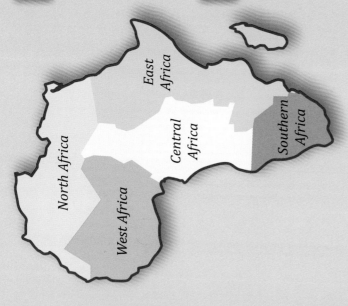

North Africa

East Africa

West Africa

Central Africa

Southern Africa

Sub-Saharan

Another geographical term used when talking about places in Africa is sub-Saharan. This is used to refer to the countries south of the Sahara Desert and below North Africa.

North Africa

Sub-Saharan Africa

Tunisia

Morocco

Western Sahara (member state)

Algeria

Libya

Egypt

Mauritania

Mali

Niger

Sudan

South Sudan

Eritrea

Ethiopia

Djibouti

Somalia

Chad

Burkina Faso

Nigeria

Cameroon

Senegal

Sierra Leone

Guinea-Bissau

Liberia

Guinea

Cape Verde

Kenya

Burundi

Tanzania

Malawi

Seychelles

Comoros

Mozambique

Madagascar

Mauritius

Swaziland

Central African Republic

Uganda

Rwanda

Democratic Republic of the Congo

Zambia

Zimbabwe

Lesotho

South Africa

Botswana

Equatorial Guinea

Gabon

Republic of the Congo

Namibia

Angola

São Tomé and Principe

Benin

Togo

Ghana

Ivory Coast

African Union

The African Union is an organization made up of representatives from all of the countries of Africa (with the exception of Morocco). It was established in 2002 with the goal of promoting peace and **prosperity** across a united continent.

The headquarters of the African Union is based in Addis Ababa, Ethiopia.

7

Early migration and empires

For many, Africa is seen as the root from which all human life has grown. The oldest human bones have been discovered here. It's also home to some of the wealthiest and oldest empires and **civilizations** in the world.

The cradle of humanity

Africa is sometimes referred to as the cradle of humanity because many experts believe that all human ancestors evolved there. Over thousands of years, descendants of these people **migrated** to live in other parts of the world.

Early kingdoms and empires

Africa has seen the rise and fall of many great kingdoms and empires. Kings and leaders controlled entire regions, built fortunes, and developed trade links.

Africa's ancient kingdoms and empires

Carthage

Ancient Egypt

Ghana
Wolof
Mali
Songhay
Kanem-Bornu
Kush
Axum
Ethiopia
Ashanti
Yoruba
Buganda
Rwanda
Luba
Congo
Lunda
Malawi
Lozi
Kilwa
Monomotapa
Meri
Zulu Kingdom

Empire of Ghana
(700 C.E.–1235)

The Empire of Ghana was formed when different tribes united under the first king, Dinga Cisse. It became wealthy through gold mining and the use of camels to transport goods across the Sahara Desert. This was an important development in the history of Africa, because it opened up trade links with other nations.

What happened?
By the 1100s, the empire's power had weakened as competition for trade improved in other parts of Africa. Finally, it came under attack from neighboring empires, becoming part of the Mali Empire.

The Empire of Ghana existed more than 373 miles (600 km) northwest of modern-day Ghana.

Ghana

Modern-day Ghana

Mali Empire (1230–1600)

A strong leader, called Sundiata Keita, united the region of the Mali Empire. It covered the area of ancient Ghana, as well as parts of modern-day Mali, Niger, and Guinea.

The empire became wealthy through trade in gold, salt, and slaves. One of the most famous rulers, Mansa Musa (1280–1337), is thought by some historians to have been the wealthiest person in history.

What happened?
The empire eventually lost power through weak rulers and raids from neighboring countries.

Sundiata Keita

A portrait from the 1300s of wealthy ruler Mansa Musa holding up a gold nugget.

Ancient Egypt (3000–30 B.C.E.)

Ancient Egypt grew out of small tribal settlements that formed along the River Nile, an important source of water for growing crops. The tribes gradually unified and were governed by a pharaoh—a ruler that was thought to be both a man and a god. There were over 170 pharaohs that ruled during this period of ancient Egypt.

What happened?
The ancient civilization eventually fell under the rule of European empires, first the Greek then the Roman Empire.

The ancient Egyptians invented many things we still use today:

Paper

Pens

Keys

Locks

Toothpaste

The most famous pharaoh was Tutankhamen (1346–1328 B.C.E.), who became ruler at the age of 9 or 10, but died at the age of 18.

Slave trade

In the 600s, traders from Arabia in western Asia were shipping slaves from Africa to India, Turkey, and Persia. In the 1400s, sailors from Europe arrived and the slave trade grew. European countries had **colonies** in North and South America and shipped African slaves there to be sold to work on plantations. As a result, there are many descendants of Africans living in North and South America. The terms African-American, African-Caribbean, and African-Brazilian are ways African descendants connect with their roots on the African continent.

Mapping independence

In the 1400s, the countries and borders of Africa began changing. They were reshaped and divided up by European colonizers and settler cultures. It's only fairly recently that Africans have been able to take back control of their lands and map out their own futures.

Scramble for Africa

Europe had begun establishing small colonies in Africa in the 1400s. But by the second half of the 1800s, there was a rush to grab large areas of land—this is known as the scramble for Africa.

To avoid conflict over who could take which land, a meeting was held in which the European powers divided up the continent. This meeting was called the Berlin Conference (1884–1885). Land was carved up with a focus on trade and resources that suited Europe. The people of Africa had no say on the borders drawn over their homelands.

Africa 1914

This French cartoon of the Berlin Conference shows the German ruler dividing Africa like a cake. It's titled "everyone gets his share."

By 1914, European countries had claimed nearly 90 percent of African territory.

France		Italy			
Great Britain		Germany			
Belgium		Portugal			
Spain		Independent			

s the 1900s progressed, African ountries began gaining independence om their European rulers.

Year of Africa

1960

1960 became known as the Year of Africa. That year, 17 countries gained independence— the largest number ever in one year.

Dates of independence

- up to 1949
- 1950–1959
- 1960
- 1961–1964
- 1965–1969
- 1970–1975
- 1976–1979
- 1980+

Ethiopia was never colonized. It was invaded by Italy in 1935 and liberated in 1941.

Zimbabwe declared independence in 1980. It was previously called Southern Rhodesia, which made a unilateral declaration of independence from the UK in 1965.

Climates

Africa is the hottest continent in the world. It has five **climate** zones, but two cover most of the continent. These zones create Africa's vast area of tropical rain forest and dry deserts.

50°C

0°C

Sahara Desert

Climate zones:

- ☐ dry
- ☐ tropical humid
- ☐ humid subtropical
- ☐ marine west coast
- ☐ Mediterranean

Tropic of Cancer

Tropical rain forests

The tropical regions on either side of the equator receive high levels of sunlight and rainfall. These provide the perfect conditions for plant growth, creating areas of dense rain forest.

This diagram shows a simplified water cycle

Water falls from clouds as rain

Equator

Heat from the Sun causes water to evaporate. The water rises into the air, and forms clouds as it cools.

Tropic of Capricorn

Namib Desert

Kalahari Desert

Cooler climates

The coastal regions in the north and south of Africa experience weather that is more varied. This is because they are exposed to areas of the ocean that bring different temperatures through the movement of ocean **currents** and wind.

Deserts

The areas farther north and south of the tropics experience short, dry winters and less rainfall. In the areas where rainfall is very scarce, there are deserts. To the north is the Sahara Desert, and to the south are the Kalahari and Namib deserts.

Sahara Desert

The Sahara Desert covers most of North Africa and is the world's hottest desert. During hot summer days, the temperature can go above 122 degrees Fahrenheit (50 °C). However, at night the heat from the day rises and the temperature drops to below 32 degrees Fahrenheit (0 °C).

Droughts

Droughts occur when an area receives no rain over a long period of time. Without rain, crops cannot grow and the soil dries up.

In East Africa in 2011, Somalia, Ethiopia, and Kenya experienced their lowest rainfall levels in 60 years. This led to a long drought that affected millions of people. Harvests failed and food prices rose. People went hungry and many died from starvation.

Highland climate

High mountainous areas are known as highlands. The climate there is different from the climate in the surrounding lowlands. This is because the temperature lowers as the **altitude** gets higher.

Mount Kilimanjaro in Tanzania has freezing temperatures at its snow covered top!

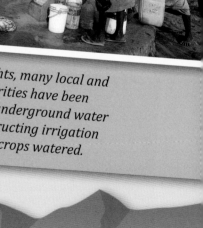

To combat droughts, many local and international charities have been building wells to underground water sources and constructing irrigation systems that keep crops watered.

The Eastern Highlands in Zimbabwe have a much cooler and wetter climate than that of the surrounding lowland.

Eastern Highlands average altitude: 3,937-5,249 feet (1,200-1,600 m).

Eastern Lowlands average altitude: 1,969-2,953 feet (600-900 m).

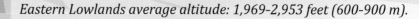
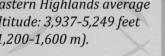

13

Wildlife

From deserts to rainforests, and **savannas** in between, Africa has a broad natural landscape that is home to some of the world's most **endangered** and deadly creatures.

Giraffe

African savanna

Savannas are stretches of grassland. The abundance of tall grass and open plains attracts grazing animals such as zebras, gazelles, and giraffes. These animals attract their predators: lions, cheetahs, and leopards.

Lion

Zebra

Grass

Savanna

Black mamba

Okavango Delta

Within the arid landscape and open savanna of Botswana is a large, wet area of land called the Okavango Delta. Most **deltas** are formed where rivers meet the sea, but the Okavango Delta is created by water from the Okavango River emptying out onto the land.

Elephant

Lemur

Okavango River

The Okavango Delta's combination of dry land and wetlands attract a wealth of wildlife, such as the rhinoceros, hippopotamus, lechwe antelope, and warthog.

Hippopotamus

Critically endangered!

frica is home to some of the world's
ost endangered animals. Many are
unted for sport, trophies, or medicines.
he effects of **deforestation** have left
any species homeless and unable to
urvive outside of their natural habitats.

*African wild
ass estimated
population: 200*

*Cross River gorilla estimated
population: 300*

*Black rhinoceros
estimated
population: 5,000*

Tiny terrors

though Africa is home to large, fierce predators,
ich as lions and crocodiles, some of its most
angerous creatures are tiny and hard to spot.

*Tsetse flies live by feeding
on the blood of animals.*

*The female
mosquito bites
into mammals to
get blood which
helps fertilize
her eggs.*

Tsetse fly

A tsetse fly bite can transmit
a disease known as sleeping
sickness. This causes a fever
and affects the nervous system.
It can be fatal if not treated.

Guinea worm

Guinea worms are disease-
spreading parasites that grow
inside humans. The adult female
worms wriggle out through the
person's skin, often through the legs
or feet. Although not deadly, guinea-
worm disease can make it difficult for
the carrier to walk. It is also very painful
when the worm exits a person's skin.

Baobabs

ere are eight species of baobab
ees, six of which can be found
Madagascar. They have huge
vollen trunks that store large
nounts of water, helping them to
rvive through periods of drought.

Mosquito

Mosquitos spread a number of deadly viruses
and diseases, such as yellow fever and malaria.
They breed rapidly in warm and wet climates,
and are very common in Central Africa.

Natural landmarks

Across Africa's large areas of desert and dense forest are giant valleys and mountains that range from the stumpy to the gigantic. This ever-changing landscape also features great lakes, breathtaking waterfalls, and a **meteorite** from outer space.

Great Rift Valley

The Great Rift Valley runs from the Middle East in Asia through to south-east Africa. Its most dramatic area of landscape is in East Africa and is known as the East African Rift. It's a natural feature that can be seen from space.

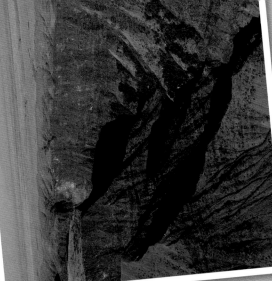

Rift valleys form when Earth's tectonic plates split apart, creating a deep trench with steep sides. The formation of the Great Rift Valley is ongoing. In a few million years, the weakening surface in the valley may cause the land in eastern Africa to split off into a separate landmass.

River Nile

The River Nile is the longest river in the world. It measures around 4,132 miles (6,650 km) in length.

Atlas Mountains

The Atlas Mountains stretch across Morocco, Algeria, and Tunisia for about 1,243 miles (2,000 km). The mountains act as a barrier, preventing moisture blown in from the Mediterranean Sea and the Atlantic Ocean from reaching the desert region.

The African Great Lakes

Tall, rugged mountains and deep lakes are located in the Rift Valley. The African Great Lakes are part of this landscape. They are:

A – Albert   **K** – Kivu   **M** – Malawi
y – Kyoga   **V** – Victoria
E – Edward   **T** – Tanganyika

River Nile

Nile Delta

Mediterranean Sea

Tunisia

Morocco

Algeria

Atlas Mountains

Sahara Desert

Niger River

Atlantic Ocean

Mount Kilimanjaro

Mount Kilimanjaro is a dormant volcano that forms part of the Great Rift Valley. It's also the highest mountain in Africa, at 19,341 feet (5,895 m).

Mosi-oa-Tunya (Victoria Falls)

The mighty Victoria Falls is located on the border between Zambia and Zimbabwe. When Scottish explorer Dr. David Livingstone stumbled across it in 1855, he was so impressed that he named it after Queen Victoria, queen of England at the time.

African Rift

A · U · Y

E · V

K · T · M

Zambezi River

Congo River

Kalahari Desert

Namibia

Namib Desert

Fish River Canyon

Fish River Canyon is the largest canyon in Africa. It's 1,804 feet (550 m) deep, 17 miles (27 km) wide, and 99 miles (160 km) long. The slopes of the canyon reveal 1.5 billion years of colorful rock formations.

Inselbergs

Knobbly inselbergs, or small single mountains, are dotted around parts of Africa. They stand alone on flat plains, and are made of tightly packed rock that is millions of years old.

An inselberg in Nigeria called Wase Rock measures 1,148 feet (350 m) in height

Hoba meteorite

The largest meteorite to have landed on Earth in one piece is in Namibia. It fell to Earth around 80 million years ago, and weighs around 66 tons (60 metric tons).

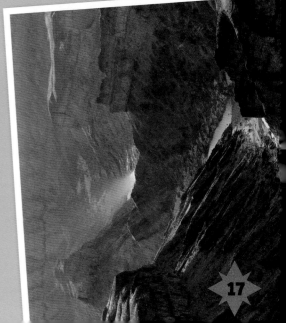

Human-made landmarks

Africa's history of ancient civilizations and colonial occupation is written in the impressive buildings and monuments that mark the continent.

The Great Mosque of Djenné

The Great Mosque of Djenné is the largest mud-brick building in the world. The walls are coated in a smooth plaster with sticks poking out.

Maqam Echahid, Algeria

Independence Arch, Ghana

Basilica of Our Lady of Peace, Ivory Coast

The first Great Mosque of Djenné was built in the 1200s. The current building dates from 1907, and is a very important site in the town of Djenné in central Mali.

The Great Enclosure

Within the country of Zimbabwe is an area known as Great Zimbabwe, once a grand royal city from the 1000s to the 1400s. Today, all that remains is a striking structure called the Great Enclosure. Its walls are as high as 36 feet (11 m), and curve 820 feet (250 m) in length.

Churches of Lalibela

Lalibela is a town in the north of Ethiopia that has 11 churches, dating from the 1100s to the 1200s. These churches were all carved out of solid rock.

The Church of St George, from Lalibela, is carved in the shape of a cross.

Egypt

Egypt

Egypt is dotted with monuments to the civilizations of its ancient history (see page 9).

Sphinx

Pyramids at Abusir ▲

Pyramids at Saqqara ▲

Pyramids at Dahshur ▲

Pyramids at Giza

Pyramids at Lisht ▲

River Nile

Luxor Temple

Parliament Building, Tanzania

Pyramids

Most pyramids were built as tombs for the rulers of Egypt and their families. To date, more than 130 pyramids have been discovered in Egypt.

The largest pyramid is the Pyramid of Khufu, also known as the Great Pyramid of Giza. When this pyramid was finished, in around 2560 B.C.E., it was 480.6 feet (146.5 m) high. For more than 3,800 years, it was the world's tallest human-made structure.

Valley of the Kings

Karnak

Abu Simbel

Settlements

The settlements in Africa range from traditional farming villages with homes that are adapted perfectly to the climate, to large modern cities—some that grew from ancient trading centers or outposts of more recent colonialism.

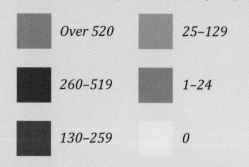

Dakar

Dakar is the capital city of Senegal. It is the most westerly point in Africa and sits on a peninsula, or a point of land sticking out into the ocean. This makes it the perfect contact point for ships sailing along the Atlantic. Today, it is one of Africa's busiest ports.

Lagos

Lagos is Nigeria's most populated city, and is the second-largest city in Africa (after Cairo in Egypt).

Lagos is divided up into 16 districts

Lagos is one of the fastest-growing urban areas in the world, with modern skyscrapers dotting the skyline. Although the city has a big network of roads, they struggle to support the growing population and rising number of vehicles.

—— *main highway*

The Maasai

The Maasai people live in parts of Kenya and northern Tanzania. They are a semi-nomadic group, which means they move from place to place but also have semi-permanent residences.

Their homes are built out of materials easily sourced from nature, such as twigs and soil. The women build the huts, and the men wrap a fence of **acacia** thorns around the settlement to keep out prowling lions.

Kenya

Tanzania

Nzulezo

zulezo is an ancient village n Ghana that is built on stilts ver Lake Amansuri. The only ay to get to the village is by anoe. The village's buildings re all connected by a series f walkways.

There are around 600 people living in Nzulezo

Industries

Africa's rich soils and resources make most of its countries centers for farming and resource extraction. African farms grow everything from grains, such as millet and wheat, to cotton and rice. Its underground mines contain precious metals and minerals.

Main industries in Africa

Crops:		Industries:		Livestock:	
Sugar		High tech		Cattle	
Corn		Mining		Sheep	
Barley		Textiles		Goats	
Oats		Timber			
Tobacco		Fishing			
Tea					
Coffee					
Rice					
Cotton					
Fruit					

Mining

Africa has one of the largest mineral industries in the world. There are underground mines all around the continent, with workers extracting precious stones such as rubies and diamonds, and metals such as gold and uranium.

Sierra Leone

Ghana

Diamonds

Sierra Leone is one of the world's largest suppliers of diamonds. This resource should make it one of the richest countries in the world, however it is one of the poorest. The country is still recovering from a brutal civil war (1991–2002), which saw a struggle for the control of diamond mines.

Gold

South Africa is the richest nation in Africa. Its mining of natural resources has been important to its economic success. It is most famous for gold mining. The country has almost 50 percent of the world's found gold reserves. It also has large coal, platinum, and diamond mining industries.

Farming

Farming is the most important industry in Africa. The crops that are grown vary depending on the climate of the region. In the tropical areas of countries such as Uganda and Cameroon, bananas, yams, tea, and coffee are grown.

Bananas

Tea

Yam

Coffee

Wheat

Millet

Barley

In the drier regions, in countries such as Chad and Sudan, cereal crops such as wheat and barley are grown.

Chad

Sudan

Cameroon

Uganda

Kenya

Madagascar

South Africa

Cotton and textiles

Small-scale farmers grow the most cotton plants, especially in the savanna areas of Africa. The production of textiles has always been a core industry in Africa, creating jobs that range from growing cotton to weaving cloth.

Kente cloth from Ghana

Sports

Sports have been played in Africa since ancient times. Today, African nations continue to produce top international sports stars in track and field, soccer, and rugby.

Mancala

For many people, mancala is Africa's national game. It's a board game played in most African countries, though its name may differ. Mancala is Arabic and means to transfer—and that is exactly what you do in the game—you move playing pieces from one cup-shaped dent to another.

Senet

Pieces of a board game called senet have been found buried in ancient Egyptian tombs dating back to 3500 B.C.E. Senet is played on a grid of 30 squares arranged in three rows of ten. Players use sets of pawns, but the ancient game's rules are unknown.

Africa Cup of Nations

Soccer is the most popular sport in Africa. Top players from African nations compete in club games around the world. Africa's own soccer tournament, the Africa Cup of Nations, is held every two years.

Nuba wrestling

Wrestling was a popular sport in ancient Egypt and in the area of Nubia, a region along the River Nile that crosses over modern-day Egypt and north Sudan. In Sudan, wrestling, known as Nuba wrestling, is still practiced today.

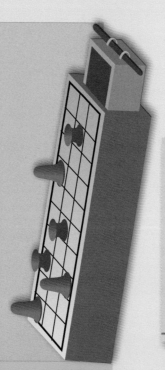

Egypt

Sudan

Ethiopia

Kenya

Rift Valley

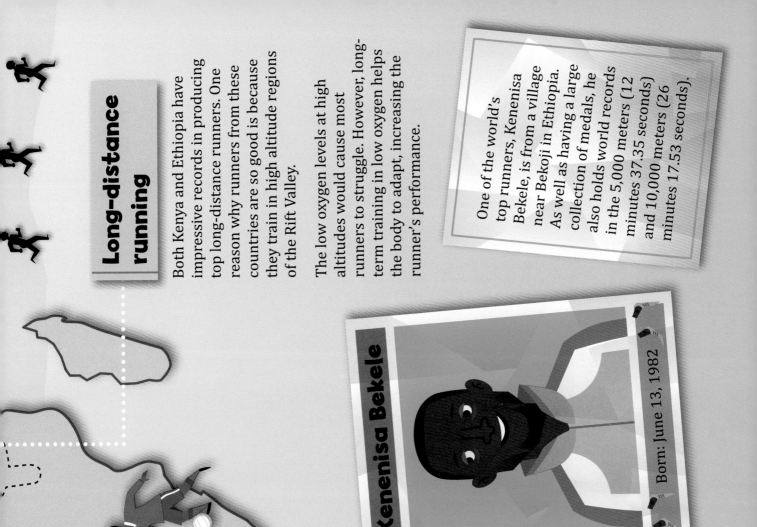

Long-distance running

Both Kenya and Ethiopia have impressive records in producing top long-distance runners. One reason why runners from these countries are so good is because they train in high altitude regions of the Rift Valley.

The low oxygen levels at high altitudes would cause most runners to struggle. However, long-term training in low oxygen helps the body to adapt, increasing the runner's performance.

One of the world's top runners, Kenenisa Bekele, is from a village near Bekoji in Ethiopia. As well as having a large collection of medals, he also holds world records in the 5,000 meters (12 minutes 37.35 seconds) and 10,000 meters (26 minutes 17.53 seconds).

Kenenisa Bekele

Born: June 13, 1982

Angola

Capoeira

Capoeira is a martial art that was developed in the 1600s by West African slaves in Brazil. It combines elements of traditional Angolan dance and acrobatics. While its popularity grew as a form of self-defense, it is now also practiced and performed around the world as a sport and a dance.

South America

Brazil

Culture

Africa's cultures are as varied as its countries and their histories. Over 2,000 languages are spoken in the continent—with 521 spoken in Nigeria alone. The continent is home to many diverse ethnic groups with their own histories and cultural traditions.

Zellige mosaics

A distinctive feature of many Moroccan buildings is the tiles that cover their walls. The zellige tile is handcrafted from glazed and fired clay that is cut into small pieces, then put together to form a large mosaic. The mosaics follow geometric patterns that can be simple shapes or complex mathematical puzzles.

Morocco

Kpanlogo dance

Kwassa kwassa dance

Burkina Faso

Benin

Nigeria

Gabon

Masks

African masks have inspired European art movements, such as Cubism, a form of abstract art. Originally created by African tribal peoples, their origins can be traced back to the Stone Age. Masks are different for each tribe.

Mask design worn by Bobo people from Burkina Faso

Mask design worn by the Fang people from Gabon

Benin bronzes

The Benin Empire controlled much of modern-day Nigeria from the 1400s to the 1800s. Inside the Benin royal palace there were hundreds of plaques, known as the Benin bronzes, decorating its walls. Most were taken by the British army during a raid in 1897. These plaques show the great skill of metalworkers and artists from the area. The bronzes portray people and events, such as important battles.

Although they are called bronzes, most of the Benin bronzes were made from brass.

Karyenda drum

The karyenda drum is a sacred instrument from Burundi, representing regeneration. It's made from hollowed tree trunks covered with animal skins. The drum is played during **rites** and rituals, such as royal coronations, weddings, and funerals.

Burundi

Large groups of drummers, such as the Royal Drummers of Burundi, produce a deep thunderous noise that has proved popular as music in its own right.

Religion

Much of Africa's traditional folk art, dance, and music have connections with tribal religions. While some of these ancient beliefs have survived, the vast majority of Africa is now dominated by Islamic and Christian faiths. These religions roughly split the continent in two: Islam in the north and east, and Christianity in the south.

Indlamu, Zulu dance

Islam

Christianity

Food and drink

African food represents its many cultures, religions, and climates. African food also reflects the influence of ancient traders, cattle cultures, and past colonial rule.

Cassava

Nigeria is the world's largest producer of cassava, one of the most important foods in Africa. The plant grows well in humid climates and can also survive in dry, drought-affected soil better than most crops. It's grown for its fat roots, which are often dried and ground into flour. It is used to make bread and dishes such as tapioca.

Spices

Spices play an important part in Moroccan food. They are sold at markets, known as souks, where they are piled high in large sacks and tubs. Bright colorful spices, such as cumin, paprika, and saffron, are used to flavor stews as well as desserts.

Tsebhi

Tsebhi is a traditional Eritrean stew made with beef or lamb. Its spicy, bittersweet flavor comes from a herb mixture that includes ginger, cloves, fenugreek seeds, and chilies.

Himbasha bread

Tagine pot, used for cooking stews, also called tagines

The cassava plant is not a native African plant. It comes from South America and was introduced to Africa by

Fufu

dish made from corn flour

Fufu is an African dish popular in Ghana. It's a sticky dough-like ball that is served with soups. It's made by boiling yams, plantains, or cassava until soft, then pounding them into a paste.

Braai

On September 24, South Africans celebrate National **Heritage** Day. On that day, the country recognizes its culture and history. Many people celebrate by having a braai—the Afrikaans word for "barbecue." A braai is considered an important part of South Africa's culture. In fact, many people now refer to National Heritage Day as National Braai Day.

Gonimbrasia belina moth caterpillars (edible)

Biltong

Biltong is a traditional South African snack of strips of dried, cured meat. Biltong is usually made from beef, but can also be made from impala, wildebeest, or ostrich meat.

29

Further information

COUNTRY	SIZE SQ MI*	POPULATION	CAPITAL CITY	MAIN LANGUAGES*
Nigeria	356,668.7	181,562,056	Abuja	English
Ethiopia	426,372.4	99,465,819	Addis Ababa	Amharic, Oromo, Somali, Trigrigna
Egypt	386,661.8	88,487,396	Cairo	Arabic
Democratic Republic of the Congo	905,354.4	79,375,136	Kinshasa	French
South Africa	470,693.1	53,675,563	Pretoria, Cape Town, Bloemfontein	Afrikaans, Northern Sotho, English, Southern Ndebele, Swazi, Xhosa, Zulu
Tanzania	365,754.4	51,045,882	Dodoma	Swahili, English
Kenya	224,080.9	45,925,301	Nairobi	English, Kiswahili
Algeria	919,595	39,542,166	Algiers	Arabic
Uganda	93,065.3	37,101,745	Kampala	English
Sudan	718,722.7	36,108,853	Khartoum	Arabic, English
Morocco	172,413.8	33,322,699	Rabat	Arabic, Berber
Ghana	92,098.1	26,327,649	Accra	English
Mozambique	308,642.2	25,303,113	Maputo	Portuguese, Makhuwa
Madagascar	226,657.7	23,812,681	Antananarivo	Malagasy, French
Cameroon	183,568.3	23,739,218	Yaoundé	French, English
Ivory Coast	124,503.6	23,295,302	Yamoussoukro	French
Angola	481,353.4	19,625,353	Luanda	Portuguese
Burkina Faso	105,869.2	18,931,686	Ouagadougou	French
Niger	489,191.2	18,045,729	Niamey	French
Malawi	45,746.9	17,964,697	Lilongwe	Chichewa, English
Mali	478,840.6	16,955,536	Bamako	French, Bambara
Zambia	290,587.3	15,066,266	Lusaka	English, many Batu languages
Zimbabwe	150,872.1	14,229,541	Harare	Shona, Ndebele, English, Tonga, Tswana, Chewa
Senegal	75,954.8	13,975,834	Dakar	French
Rwanda	10,169.2	12,661,733	Kigali	Kinyarwanda, French, English
South Sudan	248,776.7	12,042,910	Juba	English
Guinea	94,925.9	11,780,162	Conakry	French
Chad	495,755	11,631,456	N'Djamena	French
Tunisia	63,170.1	11,037,225	Tunis	Arabic
Burundi	10,745.2	10,742,276	Bujumbura	Kirundi, French
Somalia	246,200.6	10,616,380	Mogadishu	Somali, Arabic
Benin	43,483.6	10,448,647	Porto-Novo	French, Yoruba
Togo	21,924.8	7,552,318	Lomé	French
Eritrea	45,405.6	6,527,689	Asmara	Tigrinya, Arabic, English
Libya	679,361.9	6,411,776	Tripoli	Arabic
Sierra Leone	27,699	5,879,098	Freetown	English
Central African Republic	240.535.4	5,391,539	Bangui	Sangho, French
Republic of the Congo	132,046.9	4,755,097	Brazzaville	French
Liberia	42,999.8	4,195,666	Monrovia	English
Mauritania	397,955.3	3,596,702	Nouakchott	Arabic
Namibia	318,260.8	2,212,307	Windhoek	English, Afrikaans
Botswana	224,607.1	2,182,719	Gaborone	English, Setswana
The Gambia	4,363	1,967,709	Banjul	English
Lesotho	11,720.1	1,947,701	Maseru	Sesotho, English
Guinea-Bissau	13,947.9	1,726,170	Bissau	Portuguese
Gabon	103,346.8	1,705,336	Libreville	French
Swaziland	17,364	1,435,613	Lobamba, Mbabane	Siswati, English
Mauritius	787.6	1,339,827	Port Louis	Creole, English
Djibouti	8,957.6	828,324	Djibouti City	French, Arabic
Comoros	862.9	780,971	Moroni	Shikomoro, Arabic, French
Equatorial Guinea	10,830.5	740,743	Malabo	Spanish, French
Western Sahara	102,703.1	570,866	Laayoune	Arabic
Cape Verde	1,557.1	545,993	Praia	Portuguese
São Tomé and Principe	372.2	194,006	São Tomé	Portuguese
Seychelles	175.7	92,430	Victoria	French, English, Seychellois Creole

*To arrive at square kilometer (sq km), divide a number in square mi (sq mi) by 0.386102.

*There are thousands of languages that ha[ve] survived from the tribes of Africa's pre-colonial era. While not listed as being a main language of any country, many are still in use.

Glossary

acacia
a thorny tree that grows in warm countries, with yellow or white flowers

altitude
the height of something measured in relation to a given point, such as sea level

civilizations
communities that are well-organized with advanced social developments, often forming the basis for later nations

climate
average weather conditions in a particular area

colonies
countries or areas controlled by another country and occupied by settlers from that country

currents
bodies of water or air continually moving in the same direction

deforestation
the cutting down and removal of trees in a forested area

delta
a triangular-shaped piece of land that is formed when a river splits into smaller rivers, usually before it flows into an ocean

endangered
at risk of extinction, or dying out

equator
an imaginary line drawn around Earth separating the Northern and Southern hemispheres

hemisphere
half of a sphere, such as the sections of Earth divided by the equator

heritage
where you have come from, including items of historical importance and traditions from the past

member state
an area or state that is part of a political, economic, or trade organization; Western Sahara is currently part of Morocco and is not yet recognized as an independent country

meteorite
the name for a piece of rock from outer space that has landed on Earth

migrated
traveled from one region to another to live

prosperity
the state of being successful, especially in terms of making money

rites
religious acts or traditional ceremonies that mark special occasions, such as baptisms and funerals

savannas
large flat areas of land in tropical regions with a lot of grass and few trees

tropics
the two imaginary lines above and below the equator, and the region inside this area, which is the hottest part of the world

Index